God's Basketball

God's
Basketball

Brodrick Hampton

iUniverse, Inc.
New York   Bloomington

God's Basketball

iUniverse books may be ordered through booksellers or by contacting:

iUniverse
1663 Liberty Drive
Bloomington, IN 47403
www.iuniverse.com
1-800-Authors (1-800-288-4677)

ISBN: 978-1-4401-4354-0 (sc)
ISBN: 978-1-4401-4355-7 (ebk)

Printed in the United States of America

iUniverse rev. date: 04/15/2010

To my Mother and Grandmother,
who fed my love of books

and

To my Uncle John,
who encouraged me to think
and most importantly,
to question.

Contents

Acknowledgments

Without God, nothing in my life would have been possible. I am an imperfect servant, and yet He sees fit to grace me with His presence and provide all that I have…He has my eternal thanks.

My Mother and my Grandmother first introduced me both to God and to books; my love of reading books is what eventually led me to write them. I have also been blessed to have several "surrogate families": The Jenkins, the Cagles, the Fries, and the Whites, among others. This extraordinary group of "extended relatives" helped reinforce the principles, affection, and constructive experiences that my biological family provided, and laid the foundation for the positive aspects of the man – and the writer – I am today. All of you have my gratitude and my love.

Kenya, this work would not have existed without you. You alone encouraged me when this book was nothing more than an idea. Your intelligence, wit, and wisdom are true treasures in this world, and I will always remember you.

Roger, you have stood by me without fail, through both the fun times and the tough times…you are my brother.

Dianne S., you've selflessly devoted yourself to helping so many people…there are countless students who, like me, owe their success and achievements to you. If our school systems were filled with people like you, we would have better citizens and better people.

Mr. "Cadillac" – you helped me better understand ideals and that there is frequently a difference between what *should be* and what *is*…that understanding is what led to the birth of this book. You are truly unforgettable.

Scotty, you are not only my friend, but also a current-day "techno-mage." It's true that pen and paper are really all a writer needs…but with all my revisions, insertions, deletions, and re-revisions, a computer is really helpful at catching all those thoughts in my head as they tumble out. Thank you so much for helping keep all my technology – and me – running.

Mari, my fellow writer: I have always written for myself; you started me on the path toward writing for others, and I'll always remember you for that.

And last but certainly not least: Chris C., you are both a true artist and entertainer. You first showed me how to dream big and shoot for the moon.

Preface

Consider the following: a brawl between athletes...humorous antics at the announcer's table as referees attempt to sort things out...a thrown cup of ice...a fracas that winds up in the stands amongst the spectators. You might think this whole thing was a performance from World Wrestling Entertainment or one of its fellow professional-wrestling organizations. But November 19, 2004, will go down in basketball infamy as the night one simple foul became a large-scale brawl.

During the game in question, one of the team's guards fouled the opposing center with just forty-six seconds remaining in the game. The center angrily began a shoving match with the guard, which prompted a flurry of activity from the other players, officials, and coaches attempting to separate the two men and dissolve the quarrel.

Such incidents, although undesirable, are not unheard-of in professional basketball...in fact, the guard involved had left the game to recline on the scorers' table, jokingly donning an announcers' headset and waiting for the disturbance to subside. The real storm came when an irritated fan hurled a large soda cup – drink, ice, and all – at the guard on the table. Infuriated, the guard charged into the stands in the direction of the projectile's source, eventually attacking the fan he assumed to be guilty of the deed. One of the guard's teammates rushed into the stands to assist and was met by additional spectators, who promptly began trading blows with the newcomer. At this point personnel from both teams raced into the stands to separate the players and the fans in what had become an all-out melee.

Players and coaches managed to get the two men extricated from the stands, but the story didn't end there. Another fan on the floor aggressively approached the guard on the players' way out, and the guard responded preemptively by striking the fan in the face. As the man reeled, two of his teammates knocked out a second fan who ran up to join the fray. Eventually the players were hustled off the court, to a chorus of boos and a shower of drinks, cups, and debris from the remaining spectators. Everyone connected with the sport of basketball – players, fans, coaches and commentators – described the incident as one of the most shocking and infamous events ever to occur in professional basketball…most likely in the sport of basketball at *any* level. The sheer breadth and scope of the altercation alone, the likes of which had not been seen before in the NBA at the time, helped make it notable. Some of the players involved were handed record-setting suspensions, and several charges were handed down from the district attorney's office.

The names of the teams, players, fans, and coaches involved in the incident aren't mentioned here, because they're irrelevant. The fact that such an incident occurred is enough to trigger a closer look at the sport. Through personal recollection of my own limited experience as a basketball official, as well as a little research, I was able to find other altercations of a similar, if somewhat less spectacular, nature. But more and more frequently, it seems, we find ourselves shaking our heads in disbelief upon hearing about other such events happening.

Physical confrontation is not the only disgrace that has recently blemished basketball. In 2007, a referee at the highest level of the sport pleaded guilty to federal charges related to passing along inside information on NBA games for professional bookmakers. Some of the games in question were among those he personally officiated and therefore could potentially affect their outcome.

The widespread and varied nature of these happenings is a symptom of a larger problem with basketball, a problem I believe the time is right to address. The world as a whole has strayed away from the true nature of basketball: what it is, what it means, and what its purpose is for us as players, coaches, officials, and spectators. This book is an attempt to remedy this issue.

My experience as a basketball official was the original inspiration for this work. Throughout my seven-year stint of being a basketball official for high schools and various organizations, I was often amazed at the level of sportsmanship, camaraderie, courage, and dedication that players, coaches, and fans exhibited. However, I was also frequently astonished at acts of discourtesy, rudeness, intolerance, and even dishonor. Of particular concern to me was the reaction to basketball officials...it didn't seem to matter to fans, coaches, and players that officials were impartial judges and really didn't care who won or lost.

Of course, some of those reactions are simply due to bias: no one is really happy about a call that, although correct, goes against their team at a critical juncture in the game. But my main thought was that much of the grief that the sport and its officials suffered was due to frustration. Fans, coaches, and players did not always know the rules as well as officials, and those that did were often unhappy with how we had been trained to interpret them. I thought that writing something that offered people a better sense of understanding about the game, its rules, and our perspective as officials might improve things. I started the draft many times, but I could not focus on exactly what I wanted to communicate. I became discouraged and set the project aside. During that time period, I became very busy and other things crowded into my life, pushing basketball officiating to the background, and then finally, out entirely.

After some time had passed I encountered a very conservative, religious woman talking about not letting her child play certain team sports – basketball in particular – because the atmosphere around the game and its spectators was "too worldly." I remembered disagreeing with her opinion, irked by her statement. "How can she say that?" I fumed to myself. "God made basketball, too!" It was that angry flash of revelation that made me take my project off the shelf and begin looking at things with a fresh perspective. What exactly is basketball? If God DID create basketball, what is its purpose?

After some reflection and prayer, the thoughts in this book just poured out, seemingly from nowhere. Looking at this manuscript now, years later, it is very different from what I originally set out to write. But I have become convinced that this message is a step towards setting basketball back on its proper path, and it will take all involved: coaches, players, officials, and fans.

I consider myself to be a less-than-ideal herald for this message. I'm most certainly no "wise man," I am not particularly gifted with any special insight or special abilities, and I definitely don't consider myself to be any sort of spiritual authority on anything. There are numerous other people with stronger religious and spiritual credentials, and even more people possessing much greater experience with the sport (officiating or otherwise) than I have. However, I believe that the message outlined in this book can only help the sport of basketball, and hopefully give something back to the game that has provided me with so much enjoyment throughout my lifetime.

WHAT IS BASKETBALL?

Almost everyone knows about basketball, but in reflecting upon what basketball truly is, I wanted to get a working definition of the sport to start with. On impulse, I turned to one of my favorite dictionaries—*The American Heritage Dictionary (Second College Edition)*. It defines basketball as:

> **A game played between two teams of five players each, the object being to throw the ball through an elevated basket on the opponent's side of the rectangular court.**

That's a good, concise definition…but it is an earthly definition. In trying to make sense of the game from a Godly perspective, we have to go beyond the mere earthly definition of the game. We have to ask, "*Why is basketball here?*" or "*Why was basketball brought into existence?*"

All things were created by God

First of all, in attempting to answer those questions, it is important to begin with the understanding that *regardless of how a thing was created, all things have God as their source—everything came from God.* The Bible tells us from the very start:

> **In the beginning God created the heaven and the earth**
> **Genesis 1:1 (KJV)**

The scriptures in Genesis continue from that point to catalogue the various things God did during the Work of Creation: He made the Day and Night, He made the heavens and the stars in them, He made the oceans and lakes below the heavens, as well as the land, and so forth. However, John 1:3 reveals that Creation goes farther and deeper than just those opening few days catalogued in Genesis:

**All things were made by Him;
and without Him was not
anything made that was made.
John 1:3
(KJV, emphasis added)**

That means that *everything* in Creation…not just the things created at the beginning, but also the things that are being created today—technology, businesses, new kinds of cars, medicines, buildings— *all came from God.* The ideas that man had for all of the things you see in the world today—including basketball—those ideas and the things spawned by them originated from God. Everything that exists came from God.

The Misuse of Creation

"Hold on," you may say. "Look at the drugs being sold on our street corners…the guns being carried by our schoolchildren. You can't tell me God made all that!" I've actually heard similar sentiments from quite a few people, Christians and non-believers alike. But I believe those people aren't examining things closely.

The Bible speaks of the Enemy, Satan, who is in direct opposition to God and His Work. But Satan, while God's adversary, cannot do all of the things God can do. *Foremost among all, he cannot create…he can only alter and corrupt that which is already created.*

Medicine is an excellent gift from God that allows us to help heal the sick and repair the injured. Satan corrupted that tool by prodding us to alter it for purposes it was not originally designed for, and tempted us with complete dependency on it, removing our dependency on God. The result: so-called "recreational drugs" like crack and heroin, and addicts that are so dependent upon these drugs that they can cause the ruin of their lives and the lives of those around them.

Guns are remarkable tools that have protected us from the dangers of nature; and through their use in hunting, they have provided us with food and material for clothing. The Enemy tempted us to turn those same guns on each other…

and unfortunately, we did. Now a useful tool for protection and providing food has also become corrupted into a well-known instrument of fear and destruction.

There are many other examples, but these few should make it clear that nothing originally came from Satan. The Enemy cannot create a thing; he can only corrupt—or encourage us to corrupt—that thing. From that, we come to the logical realization that *while all things come from God, we may not be utilizing those things in a Godly manner.*

Basketball as God's Creation

"So what does all this have to do with Basketball?" you may ask. "Basketball is nothing more than a game!" Yes, basketball is a game...but it is something—just like everything else—that came from God.

Just for thought's sake, let's look again at our scripture from John: "*All things were made by him; and without him was not any thing made that was made.*" (John

1:3 KJV). God *never* does anything or creates anything without a purpose or plan...even though that purpose or plan may not be readily evident to us. If all things come from God, it would follow that all things—yes, even basketball—have a purpose.

Why is basketball here? One of the fastest ways to find an answer to that question is to expand on it: Why is *anything* here? Why am I here? Why are you here? Why did God create us and all of this around us? The biggest answer to that is simple: God created us for His glory.

All of us desire recognition in some form, shape, or fashion for our works. If you accomplished a difficult task at work or school, wouldn't you want the credit for it? If you created a masterpiece painting, wouldn't you want to be able to sign your name on the bottom and have that work recognized as yours? God is no different. He wants us to recognize Him as the Creator of all things and the Savior of Humanity, and to give Him the credit—*glorify* Him—in our daily life.

Thine, O LORD, is the greatness, and the power, and the glory, and the victory, and the majesty: for all that is in the heaven and in the earth is thine; thine is the kingdom, O LORD, and thou art exalted as head above all. Both riches and honour come of thee, and thou reignest over all; and in thine hand is power and might; and in thine hand it is to make great, and to give strength unto all. Now therefore, our God, we thank thee, and praise thy glorious name.
1 Chronicles 29:11-13 (KJV)

The totality of Creation was brought about to fulfill this one over-arcing, ultimate objective: to glorify God. The book of Romans sums up this thought perfectly:

For of him, and through him, and to him, are all things: to whom be glory for ever. Amen.
Romans 11:36 (KJV)

Of Him are all things: everything has Him as their sole, eternal Source. *Through Him* are all things: it is only by Him and because of Him (through His design, will, and effort) that all things are brought into existence. *To Him* are all things: everything points back to Him. Like a gift that you give "to someone," God's Creation is "to Him" in the sense that it is, in the end, *FOR* Him; its purpose being the ultimate manifestation and witness of His glory and perfection—a design present in all of His Work, from beginning to end.[1]

Everything in God's work is a testimonial to His glory—and that includes basketball.

The Purpose of Basketball

By now you're probably saying, "OK, so maybe God made basketball for His glory. But exactly how could a game fit into glorifying God?"

---

1   Adapted from the Jamieson-Fausset-Brown *Commentary Critical and Explanatory on the Whole Bible*. The original is in the public domain and may be freely used and distributed.

In answering that question, one has to consider the nature of the game. It is interesting to note that basketball is like a mirror image of life. Consider: in basketball you can do some things on your own, like facing that opponent one-on-one in a drive for the basket…but a great deal of the time we have to work with our teammates (as in life, with neighbors, friends, and co-workers) to produce better results. Also like life, basketball has conflict: there are two opposing sides working directly against each other to accomplish an objective. Basketball has rules (like laws) and officials who enforce them (like government authorities and police)…and we have to obey the rules or suffer the penalties. And in basketball—as in life—there is no guarantee that following the rules will automatically lead you to a victory.

Also, note that basketball is not just a mirror of life, but it is also an *expression* of life. Each game has its own "lifetime": a beginning, a span of time in which it is played, and an end. Just as in life, when we use our age to generally gauge our personal span of time, in basketball you can look at the game clock and estimate how much time you have left...but you never know what may happen. You might get injured, or foul out, or get removed from the game early. But one thing is certain...eventually, the game will end. And, just as in your life, your efforts and actions in the game will stand long after you leave the court, and you will be remembered by them.

In considering all of this, an interesting conclusion begins to surface. Basketball, as a reflection and expression of life, also provides us with *a Godly model for properly living life*, using the Christian principles the game is based upon. One key illustration of this is provided in the parallel between conflict in basketball and conflict in life. Because of Humanity's fall through Adam and Eve, God knew that life in this world would be imperfect. He knows that there will be disagreements, even among His children, where you will find yourselves on opposing ends of one thing or another. It may be that you and a friend are competing for the same job opportunity at work...or it may be that you disagree on a particular political or community issue.

In basketball, God provides us with a very appropriate model for handling these situations as befitting His children. We play hard for our side, to the best of our ability. We play fair. We show sportsmanship to our opponents...even though they are on "the other side," they are still human beings—still our brothers and sisters in Creation. And when the game is over, we shake hands to reaffirm our unity and friendship, recognizing that in most contests there must be a winner and a loser, that we did our best, and that there is always next time—and another chance for us to improve ourselves, regardless of whether we won or lost. It is interesting that God told us that we are to be "like a child" in our walk of faith (Matthew 18:1-3)...and a Godly model for handling our disputes lies in a *game!*

When looking at the sport from that perspective, it's significant to note the number and diverse types of people who are involved in any regulated game of basketball: two teams, each with five players plus reserves, a complement of coaches, several officials (timers, scorekeepers, referees), and any number from one to several hundred spectators. But basketball reaches far beyond that. From the players on the neighborhood court playing "street ball" to the young boy practicing his dribbling skills in his driveway; from the avid fan of any college or professional team down to the devoted parents who put up a basketball goal in the backyard for their daughter…basketball touches many lives indeed! It's as if the game were tailor-made for its message to reach almost anyone.

With that in mind, we can look at all of the participants in basketball, note their roles, and condense God's plan for basketball down into a few basic principles for each role.

Basketball is an arena where:

- **Players** can display their God-given attributes and talents in a physical testimony to Him, as well as illustrate the Christian principles inherent in the game…particularly in handling conflict.

- **Coaches** have the opportunity to mold the minds of their players into a Christian mindset, through their example and instruction in the Christian principles and values that the sport is based on.

- **Officials** have the honor of being representatives of the spirit of the game and, through enforcement, setting the standard for performance.

- **Spectators** are witnesses to the physical testimony of the players and the leadership of the coaches, with the goal of taking the principles and lessons they observe from the game and using them in their everyday life.

In the following chapters, we'll take a closer look at each of these.

THE PLAYERS OF THE GAME

If basketball were a living creature, the players would be its heart. These days one can see a lot of emphasis being placed on coaches—we hear of situations where coaches are hired at remarkable salaries, or where a coach who has had close to a decade of winning experience is released after one or two losing seasons. And yes, coaches are very important. Coaches instruct players in game principles, refine their physical techniques, and provide strategies. But the operational performance of these principles, techniques, and strategies fall to the players. It is through the endeavors of the players that a basketball game is won or lost. To put it very simply, without players there can be no game.

Players have an excellent opportunity to use their role in the game of basketball to glorify their Creator. Because they are basketball's centerpiece, players— and their performance—are in the spotlight. Players have the ability to let us as spectators see one of the marvels of God's creation—the human body—when put through physical, athletic trials demanding peak performance. At the same time, players have the chance to provide spectators with a "living illustration" of the Christian principles that form the basis of basketball, particularly in dealing with conflict.

The Human Body as God's Creation

The human body is an incredible machine. Its design enables it to perform spectacular physical feats of strength, speed, and agility. How many times have we oooohed and aaaahed at Michael Jordan's high-flying dunks...and in the face of physical resistance from his opponents, no less? Basketball is replete with similar legends who have made us gasp in amazement and awe over the years: Bill Russell, with his incredible defensive dominance…Jerry West's inexplicable "clutch shots" made under pressure…Larry Bird's dead-eye aim from three point range…Magic Johnson's remarkable "no-look" passes and assists…Shaquille O'Neal's strength and power under the basket… Allen Iverson's speed and agility in his drives to the goal. The actions of these and many, many other players are all remarkable athletic testimonies to the magnificence of design in the human body— evident because God is the Designer!

Players have a very unique opportunity to provide a visual testimony to God's design of the Human body by providing us with a look at its capabilities when pushed to its ordinary limits—and beyond. Players can accomplish this best by taking care of their bodies. The scriptural maxim about the body being the Holy Spirit's temple should have special meaning to any athlete!

What? know ye not that your body is the temple of the Holy Ghost which is in you, which ye have of God, and ye are not your own? For ye are bought

**with a price: therefore glorify
God in your body, and in your
spirit, which are God's.
1 Corinthians 6:19-20 (KJV)**

It is an athlete's responsibility to take care of his body and mind through a combination of exercise, diet, practice, and rest so that he can perform his on-court obligations to the best of his ability. That means using caution and moderation in one's choices of entertainment and activities—staying up to party with friends until 3 AM on the day of the big game will not help a player's performance that evening! And to an athlete, abusing alcohol and drugs is truly a sacrilege…as it should be to all of us!

Players' efforts on the court are born from discipline, physical fitness, and practice. They can inspire us to reach for their ideal in our own physical endeavors.

Handling Conflict: Sportsmanship

As mentioned before, part of God's plan for basketball is to provide us with a positive model for living life, through the Christian principles inherent in the game. Of particular interest to players should be how to handle the conflict that is also inherent within the game: honorably, in brotherly love and with fairness...in a word, with sportsmanship. Just as in basketball, in life sometimes we are forced to compete, and basketball shows us that we can compete in a fashion that befits us as God's children. Players are the key actors in this particular drama. It is a player's attitude towards his opponents that sets the tone for the entire game...for good or ill.

As a basketball official, I have seen the level of sportsmanship effect the game in both negative and positive ways. There are games where the spirit of play is wrong: things get too aggressive, the wrong remark is spoken, the wrong gestures made. Even if penalized by the officials, these actions can still have an effect. The next thing you know, the tone of the entire game has turned ugly, with anger bubbling just beneath the surface.

I've also been an official at games where sportsmanship was key: players took the time to help an opponent up off the floor, outstanding performances by opposing team members were acknowledged, and host coaches took the time to make the visiting coach and his team feel "at home." Everyone seemed to be having a great time. Frankly, I have always found those games to be a joy to officiate and no less exciting than games where unsportsmanlike—un-Christian—conduct threatened to ruin the experience for all involved.

Some may disagree with this. "We want to get under their skin," is what I've heard a few players and coaches say in encouraging antagonistic, unsportsmanlike behavior. But things done to harass or provoke your opponents can come back to haunt *you*, as well. Unsportsmanlike and dishonorable conduct can cause things to quickly escalate into a very unpleasant situation for everyone, with the focus of the game shifting to retribution, rather than where it belongs: on striving to excel.

Even when looking at things from a worldly standpoint, it is far better to concentrate on improving your own performance and practicing the little courtesies that make up sportsmanship—and quite possibly gain goodwill from your opponents in return—than to be inconsiderate or deliberately antagonize. However, it should be noted that under the spirit and the rules of basketball, you are expected to render sportsmanship to your opponents even if they do not render it to you in return. That is exactly what Christ asks of us as his followers:

> **Ye have heard that it hath been said, Thou shalt love thy neighbour, and hate thine enemy. But I say unto you, Love your enemies, bless them that curse you, do good to them that hate you, and pray for them which despitefully use you, and persecute you; That ye may be the children of your**

Father which is in heaven: for he maketh his sun to rise on the evil and on the good, and sendeth rain on the just and on the unjust.

Matthew 4:43-45 (KJV)

Players should dedicate endeavors to God's glory first

When a basketball player makes a conscious affirmation within his heart before each game to play "as unto God," and not simply for himself, he will achieve much more than he could ever achieve otherwise, for two reasons.

First, God will be their inspiration. If I know I'm doing something for myself, then I tend to be a little more relaxed with it…it's for me, so I can afford to be more forgiving with the results. On the other hand, if I'm doing something for someone else that I care about, I tend to take more pains with it: I want them to be pleased with the final results.

How much more so will a player take pains with his efforts if he dedicates his endeavors to God? That alone should inspire a player and cause him to "dig deeper," as the saying goes—to reach for a level of play at the peak of his performance.

Second, God will bless that performance. If a player truly dedicates his endeavors to the glorification of God, He will see that dedication, and honor it by blessing the performance—and the performer.

And a work performed with God's blessing on it will be extraordinary...*even though the player himself may not see it.*

As a player making this dedication to God, you may go out and have what you feel is a terrible performance...an "off-night." You make some bad judgments and cause turnovers, you can't hit a single shot, and after a few penalties it feels like the officials are watching you under a magnifying glass. Just remember that on the court, you are a player in *God's* drama! Sometimes you are meant to take a central role out on the floor, in the thick of things, helping to lead your team to victory. But it may also be possible that God intends for you to be seen, at that moment, as someone struggling to overcome difficulties beyond your control through effort and perseverance. Regardless of the case, you can still be content…because you are doing your best in the role God intended for you to play. The important things to remember are that you're doing this for *His* glory first, and that God is looking at things from a better perspective than we are. We never know just how God has positioned us to affect others' lives at any given moment. The only thing we can be certain of is that God wants us to do our very best in that situation and leave the rest to Him.

> **Whether therefore ye eat, or drink, or whatsoever ye do, do all to the glory of God… Even as I please all men in all things, not seeking mine own profit, but the profit of many, that they may be saved.**
> **1 Corinthians 10: 31, 33 (KJV)**

Does dedicating your performance to God insure your team's victory? Does it guarantee that performing your tasks will be any easier? *Absolutely not.* But it *will* give you the opportunity to have

God's blessing upon your performance…and even though it may not take shape in a form that you can immediately realize, you can be content with the assurance that you have served *His* purpose, which is not only higher than yours, but ultimately ensures your benefit as well.

THE COACHES OF THE TEAM

In the original *Star Wars* trilogy, Luke Skywalker is the hero, the Jedi Knight fated to defeat Darth Vader and help restore freedom and justice to the Republic. However, he couldn't have done it alone. Anyone familiar with the story will also recognize the names of Luke's wise old friend, Obi-Wan Kenobi, and his Jedi instructor, Yoda. These people were instrumental in providing him the guidance and training he needed to carry out his task and fulfill his destiny. Real life is no different: you also probably know someone who, at one time or another, had some sort of mentor—a person who passed on the advice and wisdom that only experience can provide.

Basketball answers this necessity by providing its players with their own mentors: coaches. In giving guidance and instruction, coaches must provide many things for their players: refinement of technique, strategies and tactics, discipline, physical conditioning and knowledge of the game. However, they are also responsible for instilling the Christian principles that make up the foundation of basketball, both through instruction and example.

The Godly Principles of Basketball

A coach should be aware of the fact that basketball is rich with the principles Christ gave us in order to live a fuller, deeper life in Him…it's just that most people don't realize it. The coach is responsible for imparting those values and the Christian philosophy inherent in the game to his players. We would not hire a coach who knew nothing about basketball fundamentals and strategy. In the same vein, we should not hire a coach without a firm foundation in the values basketball is based upon, such as perseverance and fair play.

Ask anyone about the positive things basketball teaches, and you will probably come up with a list similar to the following:

- The Value of Work
- Teamwork
- Discipline
- Excellence
- Respect for Authority
- Sportsmanship (Charity)
- Responsibility
- Persistence

In taking a closer look at these things, you'll see that every one of them is spoken of in the Bible as desired Christ-like traits…"Fruits of the Spirit," if you will. Let's take the value of work, for example. God never intended for His followers to be lazy:

The soul of the sluggard desireth, and hath nothing: but the soul of the diligent shall be made fat
Proverbs 13:4 (KJV)

In examining another trait, teamwork, we find that the majority of 1 Corinthians 12 is devoted to providing instruction for Christians on how to behave together in the body (the team!) of Christ. Although this passage uses the human body as an analogy, the principles apply equally to members of a basketball team:

For as the body is one, and hath many members, and all the members of that one body, being many, are one body, so also is Christ. For by one Spirit we are all baptized into one body... But now hath God set the members every one of them in the body, as it hath pleased him...And the eye cannot say unto the hand, I have no need of thee: nor again the head to the feet, I have no need of you. Nay, much more those members of the body, which seem to be more feeble, are necessary: And whether one member suffer, all the members suffer with it; or one member be

honoured, all the members rejoice with it.
1 Corinthians 12:12-13, 18,
21-22, 26 (KJV)

Let's look at one last example: persistence. The virtue of persistence on the basketball court is a mirror of the persistence necessary in following Christ. The Bible clearly lets us know that the Christian lifestyle is one of perseverance, of holding steadfast through adversity and maintaining faith:

And he spake a parable unto them to this end, that men ought always to pray, and not to faint;
Luke 18:1 (KJV)

The parable that follows is that of the unjust judge, who did not fear God nor man…however, because of a widow who persistently requested justice, he decided to grant her request "lest by her continual coming she weary me" (Luke 18: 2-8 KJV). The point was that God is infinitely more loving and fair than this unjust judge, and He will respond to our prayers…if we persist. Interestingly enough,

The Bible provides a number of encouragements to persevere in faith that are analogized with athletic endeavors.

> **Know ye not that they which run in a race run all, but one receiveth the prize? So run, that ye may obtain.**
> **1 Corinthians 9:24 (KJV)**

It becomes obvious that God doesn't want quitters on His team either! We are to continue, holding fast to our faith and the work that has been set before us, so that at the end, we can say with confidence:

> **I have fought a good fight, I have finished my course, I have kept the faith.**
> **2 Timothy 4:7 (KJV)**

There are numerous other examples where scripture can be directly tied to the positive principles that are inherent within the game of basketball…and in recognizing God's plan for basketball, that's no accident. It is important that a coach strive to instill these principles in their players, not only to create a better team, but also to create better human beings and better Christians.

Coaches as an Example

Instruction provides some learning, but another way a Coach instructs his charges is through example: his behavior sets the standard for his players to follow. With that in mind, coaches should behave in a manner befitting their profession as mentors, instructors, and guides. They should treat others with respect, and display manners appropriate with their station.

Right away some people reading this may get an image of some coach sitting with stiff formality on the sidelines, passionless and unresponsive…and that's not necessarily what being a coach is about either. If that *is* your style, and it works for you, then fine. However; all this doesn't mean you can't show emotion, or that you have to be crisp and formal. *It's how you show your emotions that count.*

I remember officiating a game where one of the coaches was so unhappy with a call that wasn't made, he actually stormed out—*way out*—on the court to protest during play! When I turned around, I spotted him on the court well past the three-point line, and I awarded him a technical foul as demanded by rule. He proceeded to intercept me on the way to the scorer's table, stood toe-to-toe with me, and, amazingly, cursed at me for what I'd done. I ejected him, of course, to the loud booing of the home team crowd. I was shocked that he not only would do such a thing, but that he would do it in front of his players. What sort of lesson were they learning from that experience? Is it possible that they saw this as acceptable behavior…reinforced by the fact that the fans were vocal in their disapproval of this coach being disciplined?

Again, don't get me wrong: I'm not saying that a coach should never yell, or should never show any emotion. On the contrary, I've been well known to say that I can appreciate an expressive coach, one who gets onto his players for poor performance and constantly pushes them to perform better. As a matter of fact, I think that a lot of the problems we have with temper these days come from our being bombarded with the ideal of heroes and heroines who are icemen under pressure. These "model" heroes are never overly expressive; they show inhuman emotional restraint in the face of all kinds of incredible crises. That image is both unrealistic and unhealthy.

As a coach, it is completely acceptable to be frustrated – even *angry* – at your players' performance…or yes, even at perceived inequities in how officials are controlling the game. However, *it is the manner in which we express that frustration, or anger, that is paramount.* An excellent verse addressing this issue lies in Ephesians:

> **Be ye angry, and sin not: let not the sun go down on your wrath.**
> **Ephesians 4:26 (KJV)**

From this verse we learn that anger in and of itself is a perfectly acceptable emotion at times. But in expressing our anger we should never resort to sinful behavior. The issue behind our anger should be dealt with in a constructive, positive manner.

The Wrong Goal for a Coach

So many coaches, players, and others involved in the game of basketball strive after wins, seeking victories alone as the ultimate holy grail. But like the proverbial martial-arts student who tried to grasp water tightly in an effort to seize it, pursuit of winning alone – at all other costs – will only cause true victory to slip through your fingers. A great coach recognizes what should be the real goal of basketball's participants: not to win, but to continually strive to improve. The logic of this sometimes escapes us in today's sports climate where winning is touted as "the only thing." But we should quickly realize that regardless of where players rank in terms of performance, if they constantly and relentlessly work at improving themselves, winning will eventually come of its own accord.

"Well, why is the score there at all?" some may ask. "If winning isn't important, why keep score?" Well, first of all winning *is* important, in a sense: to play any game well, you must play to win. *But the score, and even the concept of "winning" itself, is meant only to be a measure that inspires us to attain our true goal: to perform at the absolute limits of our ability, and then reach to surpass those limits.* If winning was the only thing, then once someone was crowned champion that would be the end of things. But in its role of glorifying God, basketball—indeed, all of sport—is about improvement, about seeking to be better players, better people...better Christians. This is reflected each year when records are reset, regardless of whom won last year, and the contest to find a champion begins anew. *The score—and the win—is not an end in and of itself...*and that is the key in how to regard basketball the right way, as God intended. The score is simply a measure...just as Christ's perfect life is a measure for us to live our lives up to.

THE OFFICIALS OF THE COURT

There is no other role in basketball that is more integral to the game—and inspires more controversy—than that of the official. Perhaps because I have been a basketball official, I tend to regard them and everything about them with more symbolism than most people. For example, the traditional basketball official's shirt is the "zebra" shirt with black and white stripes. Just as the home team generally wears their light-colored jerseys and the visiting team wears dark-colored jerseys, the officials' shirt, at once both light and dark, signifies that he represents both—but belongs to neither.

From a purely technical standpoint, officials are there to administer the game in accordance with the rules, thereby ensuring fair play and safety. However, from a more spiritual perspective, we can say that the officials are representatives of the spirit of the game. The rules of basketball are meant to protect the game's original intent and form…this is the soul of the game, its spirit. The officials, through their enforcement and administration of those rules, are agents of that spirit, ensuring its preservation. And since we have already recognized that basketball came from God, the spirit of the game is God's as well…which means that as an official, you are *His* representatives…agents of Christ, so to speak!

Representatives of the Game

In keeping with this premise of officials being agents of Christ and representing the spirit of basketball, it necessarily follows that officials *must* conduct themselves in a Christ-like manner. In examining any principles provided to guide an official's conduct, you will find that most—if not all—of those principles, by God's design, have their basis in Christ's example for behavior that He set for us. Officials must "keep their cool," even while everyone else is losing theirs. They must maintain their professionalism, even to those who are being very unpleasant to them. They must be firm and do the right thing, even though it may not be popular. And they must strive to be peacemakers and maintain order, even when faced with utter chaos.

Also, as representatives of the game, officials must realize that like coaches they, too, act as examples. Since they are representatives of the spirit of the sport, they must not behave in a manner that demeans basketball or the Godly purpose behind it. It sends a negative signal to players, who are supposed to be striving to perform to the utmost of their ability, when there are officials who are lackadaisical in performing their duties. And an official handling a particularly difficult participant in a firm, yet positive manner can send a strong message to players and coaches who may be having a difficult time with their counterparts on the opposing team. It can also provide spectators with a living example of Christian leadership that they can take for use into their own lives.

Authority through Service

An old saying popularized by the *Spiderman* movie and comic book franchise states that "with great power comes great responsibility." This holds true for authority, which is a type of power. The responsibility that accompanies authority lies in service…service to those under your authority, and to humanity in general. The military recognizes this principle when vesting its officers with command; their authority flows from their duty to properly lead and tend to the general welfare of their subordinates. Police derive their powers by being servants of the public and the law—it is because they are charged "to protect and to serve" the people that they are given their authority.

Spiderman wasn't the first place this principle was spoken of, however:

> **…The kings of the Gentiles exercise lordship over them; and they that exercise author- ity upon them are called bene- factors. But ye shall not be so: but he that is greatest among**

you, let him be as the young-er; and he that is chief, as he that doth serve. For whether is greater, he that sitteth at meat, or he that serveth? is not he that sitteth at meat? but I am among you as he that serveth.

Luke 22:25-27 (KJV)

Jesus further illustrated this principle in John 13 where, after the feast of the Passover, He poured a basin of water and washed His disciples' feet... despite one disciple's objections. Jesus explained afterwards:

Ye call me Master and Lord: and ye say well; for so I am. If I then, your Lord and Master, have washed your feet; ye also ought to wash one another's feet. For I have given you an example, that ye should do as I have done to you.

John 13:13-15 (KJV)

As a matter of fact, the entire, irrefutable premise of Jesus' Lordship over all Creation lies in His performance of the ultimate service for Mankind: He, being blameless, offered Himself as the supreme sacrifice for all of us.

Likewise, an official should never forget that their authority in the game flows directly from service to the players out on the court, as well as the coaches and spectators. Officials serve by ensuring that the game players and coaches are participating in—and that the spectators are witnessing—is a fair one, that the players' safety is being protected, and that everyone behaves in a manner befitting the sport and their participation in it.

Setting the Bar

Officials are responsible for maintaining basketball's integrity and preserving its intent and form. To do this, officials must know the rules. They must be thoroughly familiar with the operational principles of basketball and how the rules act to preserve those principles, so that they can interpret them correctly and consistently.

Officials must not shirk from their duties in administering the rules during a game. There are times when a call may be unpopular, but it is still the call that should be made. Anything a player, coach, or other participant does that is not within the spirit of the rules should be penalized appropriately. That doesn't necessarily mean blowing your whistle every five seconds; rather, it means using sound judgment and calling what you see…regardless of what anyone else may think.

At times I have seen officials (myself included) being belittled for taking things "a little too seriously." But those ten players out there on the court are depending upon the officials to protect the integrity of the game, maintain fairness, and ensure safety. If as an official, you don't do what you're there to do, then you aren't living up to the ideals behind the uniform—worse, you aren't living up to the spirit and ideals of the game itself. When that happens, I believe that the repercussions reach beyond that one particular game…all of basketball suffers. As a representative of the spirit of the game—*God's* game—any official should find that unacceptable.

Invisible Servants

Officials must remember that this is not "their game"...it is for the players and spectators. One of my favorite rules in the NFHS basketball rulebook states that when the basketball touches an official, it is considered to be touching the court at his location. I admit I probably have a deeper philosophical view of that than most other people: I have always taken it as a message that in the eyes of the game, the official is considered simply part of the court. That view further illustrates an official's role in representing basketball: they are part of the game's essence, much like the court or the ball...they are not there to be noticed. As opposed to players, who are there to exhibit their athletic skills (and return that glory to God), officials are not there to garner praise for "calling a great game." Officials are there to protect the spirit of the game and set the standards for performance by administering the rules—period. To paraphrase an old quote about officiating, "A good official is one who does his job so well that in the end, nobody notices."

THE SPECTATORS OF THE SPORT

In the 2008-2009 season (the latest statistics available at the time of this writing), NCAA men's and women's basketball had over 44 million people in attendance, spanning approximately 27,643 games.[2] The NBA's total attendance during the same period was over 42 million.[3] And those numbers, impressive by themselves, do not begin to account for the vast audience of spectators witnessing the magic of basketball via televised games.

It becomes readily apparent from those statistics that basketball touches many more lives that those who actually set foot on the court. Supporters and

2   www.ncaa.org

3   www.espn.com

fans of basketball are wide ranging in number and cross the globe, from every strata of society…a perfect audience to receive the message that God intended to communicate through the sport of basketball.

Seeing Basketball through new eyes

There are a number of reasons people go to basketball games: to see a loved one or family member who is playing or coaching, to see a favorite team or player, to support home-town athletes, or even just for simple entertainment. Nevertheless, the beauty of basketball lies in the fact that it is not only entertaining, but it is also educational.

We learn the value of persistence when a team refuses to give up and, despite overwhelming odds, manages to come back and snatch victory from the jaws of defeat. We learn how to better show brotherly love even in conflict when, after a particularly rough play, a player extends his hand to help a member of the opposing team off the floor. We learn how to be better leaders when we watch a coach gracefully guide his team under pressure. We learn patience in dealing with difficulties when we observe an official's professionalism in handling an angry player or a vociferous coach. Previously it was mentioned that basketball provides us with a chance to improve ourselves...but that improvement is not limited merely to the players, coaches, and officials. All spectators—from the excited parent sitting in the stands to the passionate fans cheering at home—have an opportunity to take the inspiring lessons of each game and apply them in their everyday Christian life.

Role Models vs. Idols

Today there is sort of an invisible tug-of-war going on between some famous athletes and their fans. Athletes are struggling to live "normal" lives, free from the spotlight of public attention and the tightrope of our often-high expectations of them. At the same time, fans and spectators insist on regarding athletes as role models, with a responsibility to behave in a manner that is a positive example to those who would look up to them and emulate them.

There is actually some merit to both views; neither side can assign sole blame to the other. The relationship between player and fan is like any other relationship; it is bound by responsibility that is carried by *both* parties.

Remember what a player's Godly purpose in the game of basketball is: to give a physical testimony to God's greatness through use of his abilities, and to illustrate the Christian principles upon which basketball is based. The game is specifically designed so that "all eyes are on him," as the saying goes. Attention is part and parcel of that package; the two cannot be separated. Players of the game must understand—and accept—that whether they like it or not, the spotlight of public attention rests on them. *Whether they choose to be active role models or not is up to them, but they should endeavor to behave in the manner all of us should behave—as Christians who are continually striving to do better.*

But even the best of basketball players are still human, and like us, they have their failings. This is where our responsibility as spectators and fans comes in. We are never to idolize these individuals and put them on superhuman pedestals as we frequently do; rather, we must remember that these people can, and do, fail. When that happens, we are to regard them as what they are: human beings, like us. We should not promote or seek to emulate their faults because of their status…and we should not belittle or degrade them for such failures, either. Instead, we should admire and respect them for their successes and the positive aspects of their performance.

We have a tendency to set people apart based on the amount of money they make, their level of fame, their talent, or other worldly distinctions. God isn't impressed with any of that; He looks at all of us the same. Because of that, the failings of those people are no more nor less than our own.

But the LORD said unto Samuel, Look not on his coun-

tenance, or on the height of his stature; because I have refused him: for the LORD seeth not as man seeth; for man looketh on the outward appearance, but the LORD looketh on the heart.
                    1 Samuel 16:7 (KJV)

Using what Basketball teaches

There is nothing wrong with remembering players' names, statistics, and feats of skill on the basketball court. However, we should also be striving to recognize and remember the positive values they are illustrating through their performances.

Imagine what a world it would be if everyone worked hard and tried their best...if we treated those with differing views and goals with respect...if everyone had persistence in the face of difficulty... if people took both life's victories and defeats graciously. These are just a few of the principles that basketball teaches us, by God's design...and those principles show us the life that Christ intended for us to live.

EPILOGUE

Invariably, basketball is here to stay. It has firmly stood the test of time, like good writing and good food, and it shows no sign of abating…so there is little question that it will remain. The only question lies with its future.

What will the players of tomorrow look like? What future legends will arise from their ranks? Will the sport evolve? Will goals get higher? Will periods become longer or shorter? What rules will be changed?

We can be assured that changes will come. After all, one of the final lessons basketball teaches us—not only in the rhythm and momentum within each game, but also in the records and champions over the ages—is that one of the constants in this world is change. Change is inevitable, and like everything else that endures, basketball will continue to change and adapt.

However, basketball also shows that in this life, there is another constant, and that is God. Throughout the decades, throughout the various stars who have graced the sport, throughout the various changes and additions in rules and procedures, the Christian principles and ideals that are inherent within the sport have remained constant. Just as players and fans can take heart that the essence of basketball will remain despite any changes, we can rest assured that throughout life's tumults, tragedies, and triumphs, God is ever present, ever capable, and ever loving. And, if we continue to regard basketball—God's basketball—the way He intended, we ensure our benefit from the many blessings the sport has to offer, and we can be assured that it will retain the prominence it deserves as one of the greatest games on Earth.

ABOUT THE AUTHOR

Brodrick Hampton is a Louisiana native and graduate of Louisiana State University. He officiated basketball at various levels for seven years; additionally, he has worked in such diverse fields as systems analysis, radio entertainment, and media consulting. He currently works as a writer/editor in public relations and an instructor of English, and he maintains ties to the sport of basketball through his work as a courtside announcer. Brodrick Hampton presently resides in Baton Rouge, Louisiana, and is the author of *Brodrick's Pen*, a local column and online blog.